PRESENTED TO

_____

FROM

_____

MESSIAH

COME ✤AND✤ BEHOLD HIM

MAX LUCADO
BILLY GRAHAM
CHARLES F. STANLEY
HENRY & RICHARD BLACKABY
ANNE GRAHAM LOTZ
JOHN MACARTHUR
JACK COUNTRYMAN

THOMAS NELSON
Since 1798

NASHVILLE   DALLAS   MEXICO CITY   RIO DE JANEIRO

Messiah: Come and Behold Him
© 2010 by Thomas Nelson, Inc.®

Published in Nashville, Tennessee, by Thomas Nelson. Thomas Nelson is a trademark of Thomas Nelson, Inc.

Thomas Nelson, Inc., titles may be purchased in bulk for educational, business, fund-raising, or sales promotional use. For information, please email SpecialMarkets@ThomasNelson.com.

Cover design by Koechel Peterson Design, Minneapolis, MN.

ISBN-13: 978-1-4041-8972-0

Printed in the United States of America
14 13 12 11 10 – DP – 6 5 4 3 2 1

AND HE SHALL BE CALLED

ADVOCATE Shiloh The Resurrection & The Life
Master Shiloh Judge **Lord of lords**
Shepherd & Bishop of Souls *High Priest*
Rock MAN OF SORROWS Messiah
HEAD OF THE CHURCH Teacher
Savior FAITHFUL & TRUE WITNESS Servant
LIVING WATER *Rose of Sharon*
Alpha & Omega **Bread of Life**
Mediator Holy One I Am *True Vine*
Son of God The Beloved
GOOD SHEPHERD **The Almighty**
BRANCH Light of the World
Carpenter IMAGE OF THE INVISIBLE GOD
Chief Cornerstone **The Door** Bridegroom
AUTHOR & FINISHER OF OUR FAITH
ANCHOR **The Word** Lamb of God
Everlasting Father *Redeemer*
Dayspring *King of kings* **Prophet**
LION OF THE TRIBE OF JUDAH *The Amen*
King of the Jews Only Begotten Son
Immanuel **Wonderful Counselor** SON OF MAN
Prince of Peace Bright Morning Star
THE WAY, THE TRUTH, & THE LIFE

JESUS CHRIST

PREFACE

May focusing on the names of Jesus capture your heart with the reality of how greatly you are loved by God. Learn His character. Experience His strength. Embrace His love for you. Allow this journey to penetrate your heart and empower your actions as you affirm that He does surely reign today, tomorrow, and forever and ever.

Jack Countryman

Contents

IMMANUEL

*Behold, the virgin shall conceive and bear a Son,
and shall call His name Immanuel.*

ISAIAH 7:14

I have had psychiatrists tell me their schedules are overloaded with people who find the Christmas season almost more than they can bear because of their loneliness and isolation.

Christmas is God's reminder that we are not alone. God revealed in the life, death, and resurrection of Jesus a reconciling love that rescues us from separation and loneliness. We are not alone; God has come down from Heaven to tell us He loves us!

At this Christmas season you can be assured that Jesus Christ is here. He is here to give us hope, to forgive our sins, to give us a new song, to impart faith, and to heal our spiritual wounds if only we will let Him.

If you are lonely this Christmas, welcome Christ into your life. Then ask Him to help you reach out to someone else who is lonely, and show that person His love.

BILLY GRAHAM
Hope for Each Day

CHRIST THE LORD

*There is born to you this day in the city of
David a Savior, who is Christ the Lord.*

LUKE 2:11

When the shepherds found the baby wrapped in swaddling clothes and lying in a manger, they found "a Savior who is Christ the Lord." He came as a sin offering for mankind. He came as the Savior, the fulfillment of the Old Testament prophecies as the Messiah; but He came as Lord of heaven and earth also. . . .

Jesus Christ is the ruling, reigning, sovereign Lord over all.

CHARLES F. STANLEY
God's Way Day by Day

Faithful Witness

*From Jesus Christ, the faithful witness, the firstborn
from the dead, and the ruler over the kings of the earth.
To Him who loved us and washed us from our sins
in His own blood, and has made us kings and
priests to His God and Father, to Him be glory
and dominion forever and ever. Amen.*

Revelation 1:5-6

Throughout history there has never been a more faithful witness than Jesus Christ. He was a model of servanthood and portrayed for everyone through His everlasting love how precious we are to our Father God.

We are priests in a lost world with one purpose: to glorify God and bear witness that Jesus Christ is the only answer to life everlasting. May the Holy Spirit so control our lives that we shall count it our highest privilege to manifest our Lord and Savior to a lost world. He is not only the transcendent Diety who created us, He is the One who died on our behalf and was subsequently raised from the dead—the first One who experienced the true resurrection.

Jack Countryman

13

HOPE

They shall obtain joy and gladness,
And sorrow and sighing shall flee away.
ISAIAH 35:10

The black, velvety sky was clear and studded with sparkling stars that had looked down on earth since the beginning of time. Shepherds appeared to be sitting idly by their flocks but in fact were keeping a sharp lookout for anything or anyone who might harm the sheep entrusted to their care. In the distance, the lights from the town could be seen and the noisy commotion could be heard as more people were coming into the town than the town could hold.

On the clear night air, sound traveled easily and somewhere from the direction of the village inn someone slammed a door. And a baby cried.

The seed of the woman, who would open heaven's gate and welcome any and all who place their faith in Him . . . had been given!

The hope that was born that night continues to radiate down through the years until it envelops your heart and mine.

ANNE GRAHAM LOTZ
God's Story

HOLY

*He who is mighty has done great things
for me, and holy is His name.*
LUKE 1:49

We must never forget that when we celebrate Christ and His birth, we are celebrating the God of heaven and earth.

Some may not submit to His lordship, but that doesn't change the position the Father has given His Son. Jesus is Lord whether recognized or not, and He wants to be Lord of your life.

This is the divine structure God has ordained. . . . Anytime we fail to give Christ His rightful place in our lives—first place—we can miss out on the blessings of God.

CHARLES F. STANLEY
God's Way Day by Day

Shepherd

The Lord is my shepherd;
I have everything I need.
Psalm 23:1 ncv

Sheep aren't smart. They tend to wander into running creeks for water, then their wool grows heavy and they drown. They need a shepherd to lead them to "calm water" (Psalm 23:2). They have no natural defense—no claws, no horns, no fangs. They are helpless. Sheep need a shepherd with a "rod and . . . walking stick" (Psalm 23:4) to protect them. They have no sense of direction. They need someone to lead them "on paths that are right" (Psalm 23:3).

So do we. We, too, tend to be swept away by waters we should have avoided. We have no defense against the evil lion who prowls about seeking whom he might devour. We, too, get lost.

We need a shepherd. We need a shepherd to care for us and to guide us. And we have one. One who knows us by name.

Max Lucado
A Gentle Thunder

ADVOCATE

*My little children, these things I write to you, so
that you may not sin. And if anyone sins, we have an
Advocate with the Father, Jesus Christ the righteous.*

1 JOHN 2:1

In God's perfect plan, He has chosen to provide
His Son to help us be on guard to our sinful
tendencies. When Satan charges us with sin,
Christ represents us and defends us to the Father.
His covering of our sin is manifested in all that
He does for us. We truly have an advocate that
stands in the gap every hour of every day with our
Heavenly Father. Therefore, knowing that Jesus
represents us as our advocate with the Father to
plead our cause in Heaven's court, let us live in
such a way that God will be glorified. Our spirit
will be strengthened to live boldly in a lost world
that needs to know the love of God.

JACK COUNTRYMAN

PRINCE OF PEACE

For unto us a Child is born, Unto us a Son is given;
And the government will be upon His shoulder.
And His name will be called Wonderful, Counselor,
Mighty God, Everlasting Father, Prince of Peace.

ISAIAH 9:6

Many of us find it hard to read those words without hearing Handel's *Messiah* in our mind. That magnificent music beautifully captures the glorious promise and rich truth of these ancient words.

Israel hoped for, longed for, waited for a messiah who would prove victorious over their military oppressors. Israel anticipated a messiah who would bring peace on earth.

God's Messiah—Jesus His Son—would prove victorious over a greater enemy: sin. God's Messiah would also bring a much greater peace: reconciliation between God and man.

Christ can indeed bring peace to any situation. The most difficult circumstance, the most ruthless enemy, the deepest pain—none of these is beyond Christ's reach. He can calm your heart and mind. No one brings peace like Jesus.

HENRY & RICHARD BLACKABY
Discovering God's Daily Agenda

GIFT OF GOD

*Every good action and every perfect
gift is from God. These good gifts come
down from the Creator of the sun, moon, and
stars, who does not change like their shifting shadows.*

JAMES 1:17 NCV

The conclusion is unavoidable: self-salvation simply does not work. Man has no way to save himself.

But Paul announces that God has a way. Where man fails God excels. Salvation comes from heaven downward, not earth upward. "Every good action and every perfect gift is from God" (James 1:17).

Please note: Salvation is God-given, God-driven, God-empowered, and God-originated. The gift is not from man to God. It is from God to man.

MAX LUCADO
In the Grip of Grace

Firstborn over All Creation

He is the image of the invisible God, the firstborn over all creation. For by Him all things were created that are in heaven and that are on earth, visible and invisible, whether thrones or dominions or principalities or powers. All things were created through Him and for Him.

Colossians 1:15-16

So many statements in Scripture make plain the fact that God and Christ are one. He is the manifestation of God. The invisible God has become visible to men in Jesus Christ. He is the Head of the natural creation and the new creation, so that He is intimately allied to us. Jesus Christ is the eternal One who was before all creation. The Word proclaims that "all things were created through Him," and that He is before all things. Since Christ is God, He is supreme in rank over all creation. Yet He is not only the transcendent deity who created us, He is the one who died on our behalf and was subsequently raised from the dead. Therefore He is also the firstborn from the dead, the first one who experienced the true resurrection.

Jack Countryman

SON OF MAN

For even the Son of Man did not come to be served,
but to serve, and to give His life a ransom for many.
MARK 10:45

Here's a side to the Christmas story that isn't often told: those soft little hands, fashioned by the Holy Spirit in Mary's womb, were made so that nails might be driven through them. Those baby feet, pink and unable to walk, would one day walk up a dusty hill to be nailed to a cross. That sweet infant's heat with sparkling eyes and eager mouth was formed so that someday men might force a crown of thorns onto it. That tender body, warm and soft, wrapped in swaddling clothes, would one day be ripped open by a spear.

Jesus was born to die.

Don't think I'm trying to put a damper on your Christmas spirit. Far from it—for Jesus' death, though devised and carried out by men with evil intentions, was in no sense a tragedy. In fact, it represents the greatest victory over evil anyone has ever accomplished.

JOHN MACARTHUR
Truth for Today

JESUS

Joseph . . . took to him his wife, and did not know her till she had brought forth her firstborn Son. And he called His name Jesus.
MATTHEW 1:24-25

Joseph tanked his reputation. He swapped his *tsadiq* diploma for a pregnant fiancée and an illegitimate son and made the big decision of discipleship. He placed God's plan ahead of his own.

Rather than make a name for himself, he made a home for Christ. And because he did, a great reward came his way. "He called His name Jesus."

Queue up the millions who have spoken the name of Jesus, and look at the person selected to stand at the front of the line. Joseph. Of all the saints, sinners, prodigals, and preachers who have spoken the name, Joseph, a blue-collar, small-town construction worker said it first. He cradled the wrinkle-faced prince of heaven and with an audience of angels and pigs, whispered, "Jesus . . . You'll be called Jesus."

MAX LUCADO
Cure for the Common Life

Author of Our Faith

*Looking unto Jesus, the author and finisher of
our faith, who for the joy that was set before Him
endured the cross, despising the shame, and has
sat down at the right hand of the throne of God.*

Hebrews 12:2

Everything begins and ends with Jesus. Through Him we have life. We need to consistently focus on Christ instead of our own circumstances. Christ has done everything necessary for us to endure in our faith. There will be trials, but we are to "count it all joy" (James 1:2). Step by step He goes before us and leads us on. The best is always before us and someday we will meet Him face to face and reign with Him in glory. He is our example and model, for He focused on the "joy that was set before Him." His attention was not on the agonies of the cross, but on the crown; not on the suffering, but on the reward.

Jack Countryman

Light of the World

I am the light of the world. He who
follows Me shall not walk in darkness. . . .

John 8:12

This month the birthday of Jesus Christ will be celebrated all over the world. It will be celebrated in various ways, in many languages, by people of all races. For a few hours many in the world will stop talking of satellites, rockets, and war. For a few hours they will talk of peace on earth and good will toward men. People will exchange their gifts and talk about the Prince of Peace.

Imagine the scene in Bethlehem two thousand years ago. It was the night of nights, and yet it had begun as every other night had before it.

But it was to become the greatest, most significant night of history. This was the night that would conquer darkness and bring in the day when there would be no more night. This was the night when those who sat in darkness would see a great light. This was the night God brought into the world the One who is "the light of the world." May His light shine in your life this Christmas season!

Billy Graham
Hope for Each Day

DELIVERER

And so all Israel will be saved, as it is written:
"The Deliverer will come out of Zion,
And He will turn away ungodliness from Jacob;
For this is My covenant with them,
When I take away their sins."

ROMANS 11:26–27

Seven hundred and fifty years before the birth of our Savior, Isaiah wrote of the Deliverer and Redeemer that would come out of Zion. He came with one purpose and that was to show us the way and deliver us from our sin. Through His life and sacrifice, we have eternal life that is secure and nothing or no one can ever take that away from those who choose to accept Him. Life is filled with many challenges and choices, and we are invited to live in communion with Christ. As Christ delivered Himself up as a sacrifice for our sins, let us live in such a way that each day may be filled with the power and pleasure of His presence. He has promised to deliver us from every problem we may face if we will only trust Him and lean on His shoulders.

JACK COUNTRYMAN

HIGH PRIEST

Now this is the main point of the things we are saying:
We have such a High Priest, who is seated at the right
hand of the throne of the Majesty in the heavens.

HEBREWS 8:1

The Jewish priests daily entered the sanctuary to burn incense and trim the lamps. Once a week they replaced the showbread. Once a year, on the Day of Atonement, the high priest entered God's presence. Clearly, the old covenant did not provide for full fellowship between God and His people.

The blood of Christ changed that, though. His death on the cross was the perfect and complete sacrifice for humanity's sins. In fact, no sin or offense is so great that Jesus' atonement cannot make you clean and holy.

We will face temptations and difficult circumstances. At times our strength may fail and our faith may waiver, but we have this hope: Christ our High Priest forever intercedes for us with the Father. He is victorious over death and sin, and He will bring us victory as well.

HENRY & RICHARD BLACKABY
Discovering God's Daily Agenda

REDEEMER

"The Redeemer will come to Zion,
And to those who turn from transgression in Jacob,"
Says the LORD.
ISAIAH 59:20

The Jewish prophets proclaimed that a redeemer would come out of Zion to be the Helper the people so desperately needed. Today, we are blessed that our Redeemer Jesus Christ came in the form of a man with one purpose, to redeem us from our sin.

When life seems difficult and the race we are running seems all uphill, stop and think, *our Lord redeemed us at a priceless cost.* If He saw in us enough worth for which to pay His life, is it not worthwhile to rise up and try again, walking with Him and worshiping Him who has redeemed us from our sin?

JACK COUNTRYMAN

The Living Stone

You come to him, the living Stone. . . .
Now to you who believe, this stone is precious.
1 Peter 2:4, 7 niv

Have you ever denied the Lord?

Denied Him with your silence?

Denied Him with your behavior?

Denied Him by calling yourself a Christian yet not acting like one?

Denied Him by priorities and plans and people and places in your life that are Christ-less?

If you have denied Jesus—and surely all of us have in some way—then you know something of the price Peter paid in shame and humiliation for his denial. Instead of repressing your shame and guilt, will you confess it to the Lord so that you can experience the same forgiveness and restoration that Peter did? When you do, you can share the testimony with Peter and the saints down through the ages who know from their own experience that He is precious! "Speak, Lord, for your servant is listening" (1 Samuel 3:9 niv).

Anne Graham Lotz
Just Give Me Jesus

King of Kings

The Lamb . . . King of kings.
Revelation 17:14

From his very birth Christ was recognized as King. Something about Him inspired allegiance, loyalty, and homage. Wise men brought Him gifts. Shepherds fell down and worshiped Him. Herod, realizing that there is never room for two thrones in one kingdom, sought His life.

As Jesus began His ministry, His claims upon people's lives were total and absolute. He demanded and received complete adoration and devotion. Mature men and women left their businesses and gave themselves in complete obedience to Him. Many of them gave their lives, pouring out the last full measure of devotion.

He was more than a poet, more than a statesman, more than a physician. We cannot understand Christ until we understand that He was the King of kings and Lord of lords. Like Thomas, our only response must be to bow down and confess, "My Lord and my God!" (John 20:28).

Billy Graham
Hope for Each Day

MEDIATOR

For there is one God and one mediator between God and men, the man Christ Jesus.

1 TIMOTHY 2:5

Mediator was a concept derived from ceremonial worship prescribed by God in the Old Testament. In the temple, priests mediated between God and the Israelites by offering animal sacrifices to atone for the sins of the people and by interceding to God for the nation. In their position as mediator, the priests were the only ones eligible to enter the Holy place, the place where God made His presence known. When Jesus came to us as the Son of God and shed His blood on the cross for our sins, He became our High Priest. He is the Mediator of the New Covenant by means of His death for the redemption of our transgressions, that we might obtain forgiveness and receive the promise of eternal inheritance with God. There is only one way to Him—through the Mediator, Jesus Christ—who has the full nature of God and the full nature of man.

JACK COUNTRYMAN

SAVIOR

Today your Savior was born in the town
of David. He is Christ, the Lord.

LUKE 2:11 NCV

An ordinary night with ordinary sheep and ordinary shepherds. And were it not for a God who loves to hook an "extra" on the front of ordinary, the night would have gone unnoticed. The sheep would have been forgotten, and the shepherds would have slept the night away.

But God dances amidst the common. And that night he did a waltz.

The black sky exploded with brightness. Trees that had been shadows jumped into clarity. Sheep that had been silent became a chorus of curiosity. One minute the shepherd was dead asleep, the next he was rubbing his eyes and staring into the face of an alien. The night was ordinary no more.

The angel came in the night because that is when lights are best seen and that is when they are most needed. God comes into the common for the same reason. His most powerful tools are the simplest.

MAX LUCADO
The Applause of Heaven

My Beloved Son

While he was still speaking, behold, a bright cloud
overshadowed them; and suddenly a voice came out
of the cloud, saying, "This is My beloved Son, in
whom I am well pleased. Hear Him!"

Matthew 17:5

God the Father loved Jesus the Son and publicly stated His pleasure in Christ's righteous manner of living. Jesus was totally obedient to the Father even unto death. God sent His Son to the cross on our behalf to provide for us a propitiation for our sin and a direct access to our Father God. Through this Scripture we are invited to "hear Him." Jesus, through the Holy Spirit, wishes to be our guide through life. As Jesus was in total obedience to the Father, our lives need to acknowledge Him and listen to that small, still voice that is ever-present for those who are followers of Jesus Christ.

Jack Countryman

The Way, Truth, and Life

I am the way, the truth, and the life.

John 14:6

When we become a friend of Jesus, something revolutionary happens inside us. Our spirits, our hearts, our souls, our perspectives on life, and our capacities to love all change dramatically. We become a "New Creation."

Jesus gives to us something far more valuable than any human friend can ever give: He reveals to us the truth about God . . . the truth about ourselves . . . the truth about the relationship He desires for us to have with other human beings. He reveals in His own presence within us the whole truth, and nothing but the truth. He is Truth.

Charles F. Stanley
God's Way Day by Day

LAMB OF GOD

The next day John saw Jesus coming toward him, and said, "Behold! The Lamb of God who takes away the sin of the world!"

JOHN 1:29

In the Old Testament, the Israelites sacrificed lambs at the Passover feast as an offering for their sins. Jesus Christ is the Lamb that God gave us as a sacrifice for sins not only for Israel but for the whole world. No one else could be God's Lamb. He was the voluntary offering. What can we do? Believe it, accept it, take our place with Him, behold Him every day, and count nothing as too inadequate or too little for Him. May each day bring you to the throne of Grace with an open heart to the leading of the Holy Spirit in everything you do. Let us be reminded that this vivid description of Jesus was a pointed announcement of the Atonement He would bring about on our behalf that we might have eternal life with our Heavenly Father.

JACK COUNTRYMAN

GOOD SHEPHERD

*I am the good shepherd. I know my sheep,
and my sheep know me. . . .*
JOHN 10:14 NCV

The shepherd knows his sheep. He calls them
by name. When we see a crowd, we see exactly
that, a crowd. . . . We see people, not persons, but
people. A herd of humans. A flock of faces. That's
what we see.

But not so with the Shepherd. To him every
face is different. Every face is a story. Every face is
a child. Every child has a name. . . .

The shepherd knows his sheep. He knows each
one by name. The Shepherd knows you. He knows
your name. And he will never forget it.

MAX LUCADO
When God Whispers Your Name

BREAD OF LIFE

I am the bread of life.

John 6:35

Jesus came to the world so we could know, once and for all, that God is concerned about the way we live, the way we believe, and the way we die.

God could have told us in other ways, of course—and He had, throughout the pages of the Old Testament and in the lives of His people. By His written Word He declared His love.

But Jesus was the Living Word. By His life, death, and resurrection, Jesus *demonstrated* God's love in a way we could never deny. Paul wrote, "But God demonstrates His own love toward us, in that while we were still sinners, Christ died for us" (Romans 5:8).

Every time He fed the hungry, He was saying, "I am the bread of life." Every time He healed a suffering person, He was saying, "It hurts Me to see you in pain." Every move He made, every miracle He performed, every word He spoke was for the purpose of reconciling a lost world to the loving, compassionate God.

BILLY GRAHAM
Hope for Each Day

WORD

*The Word became flesh and blood,
and moved into the neighborhood.*
JOHN 1:14 MSG

I've always perceived the apostle John as a fellow who viewed life simply. "Right is right and wrong is wrong, and things aren't nearly as complicated as we make them out to be."

For example, defining Jesus would be a challenge to the best of writers, but John handles the task with casual analogy. The Messiah, in a word, was "the Word." A walking message. A love letter. Be He a fiery verb or a tender adjective, He was, quite simply, a word.

And life? Well, life is divided into two sections, light and darkness. If you are in one, you are not in the other and vice versa.

Next question?

MAX LUCADO
No Wonder They Call Him the Savior

Alpha & Omega

*"I am the Alpha and the Omega," says the
Lord God, "who is, and who was, and
who is to come, the Almighty."*
Revelation 1:8 niv

This title describes the eternal omniscience of
Jesus Christ. The alpha is the first letter and
the omega is the last letter in the Greek alphabet.
Through the alphabet all of our words, all of our
wisdom, and all of our knowledge are expressed.
Jesus is the beginning and the end of the alphabet,
the summation of all wisdom and knowledge.

What does the omniscience of Christ mean to
me personally? It means I have always been on
His mind. Think of it: The most important Man
in the universe has always been thinking of you!
Wonder of wonders! You have never been out of
His thoughts! Even as He hung on the cross, He
was thinking of you by name! Dying for you by
name! And when He was raised from the dead on
that first Easter Sunday, He was raised with you
on His mind!

Anne Graham Lotz
The Vision of His Glory

RESURRECTION

*I am the resurrection and the life. He who
believes in me will live, even though he dies.*

JOHN 11:25 NIV

Her words were full of despair. "If you had
been here . . ." She stares into the Master's
face with confused eyes. She'd been strong long
enough; now it hurt too badly. Lazarus was dead.
Her brother was gone. And the one man who
could have made a difference didn't. He hadn't
even made it for the burial. Something about
death makes us accuse God of betrayal. "If God
were here there would be no death!" we claim.

You see, if God is God anywhere, He has to
be God in the face of death. Pop psychology can
deal with depression. Pep talks can deal with
pessimism. Prosperity can handle hunger. But
only God can deal with our ultimate dilemma—
death. And only the God of the Bible has dared to
stand on the canyon's edge and offer an answer.
He has to be God in the face of death. If not, He is
not God anywhere.

MAX LUCADO
God Came Near

MESSIAH

*The woman said to Him, "I know that
Messiah is coming" (who is called Christ).
"When He comes, He will tell us all things."*
JOHN 4:25

Throughout history the Jewish people had looked forward to the coming of the Messiah, the anointed one by God. He was to give them the Spirit of Life and hope that the Samaritan woman's lips bore. May our lips today bear a convincing, convicting, and converting testimony of the saving grace of the living Christ. May this Christmas bring to light the coming of the Messiah to show each of us the love and sacrifice of Jesus Christ. May we share with Him life eternal and experience, through His love, the joy and peace that comes with knowing Christ as our personal Savior.

JACK COUNTRYMAN

Hallelujah Chorus
from Handel's Messiah

Hallelujah! Hallelujah! Hallelujah!
Hallelujah! Hallelujah!
For the Lord God omnipotent reigneth.
Hallelujah! Hallelujah! Hallelujah! Hallelujah!

For the Lord God omnipotent reigneth.
Hallelujah! Hallelujah! Hallelujah! Hallelujah!
Hallelujah! Hallelujah! Hallelujah!

The kingdom of this world
Is become the kingdom of our Lord,
And of His Christ, and of His Christ;
And He shall reign forever and ever,
Forever and ever, forever and ever,

King of kings, and Lord of lords,
King of kings, and Lord of lords,
And Lord of lords,
And He shall reign,
And He shall reign forever and ever,
King of kings, forever and ever,
And Lord of lords,
Hallelujah! Hallelujah!

And He shall reign forever and ever,
King of kings! and Lord of lords!
And He shall reign forever and ever,
King of kings! and Lord of lords!
Hallelujah! Hallelujah! Hallelujah!
Hallelujah! Hallelujah!

GEORGE FREDERIC HANDEL (1695-1759)

Endnotes

11. *Hope for Each Day*, Billy Graham, p. 384. (Nashville, TN: Thomas Nelson, Inc., 2002).

12. *God's Way Day by Day,* Charles F. Stanley, p. 380. (Nashville, TN: Thomas Nelson, Inc., 2004).

14. *The Joy of My Heart*; Anne Graham Lotz, p. 386. Originally from *God's Story*, (Nashville, TN: W Publishing, 1997).

15. *God's Way Day by Day*, Charles F. Stanley, p. 358. (Nashville, TN: Thomas Nelson, Inc., 2004).

16. *Grace for the Moment,* Max Lucado, p. 692. Originally from *A Gentle Thunder* (Nashville, TN: Word, 1995).

18. *Discovering God's Daily Agenda,* Henry & Richard Blackaby, p. 382. (Nashville, TN: Thomas Nelson, Inc., 2007).

19. *Grace for the Moment,* Max Lucado, p. 740. Originally from *In the Grip of Grace* (Nashville, TN: Word, 1996).

21. *Truth for Today*, John MacArthur, p. 386. (Nashville, TN: JCountryman, 2001).

22. *Grace for the Moment*, Max Lucado, p. 749.
Originally from *Cure for the Common Life*
(Nashville, TN: W Publishing Group, 2005).

24. *Hope for Each Day*, Billy Graham, p. 376.
(Nashville, TN: Thomas Nelson, Inc., 2002).

26. *Discovering God's Daily Agenda*, Henry & Richard
Blackaby, p. 388. (Nashville, TN: Thomas Nelson,
Inc., 2007).

28. *The Joy of My Heart*; Anne Graham Lotz, p. 257.
Originally from *Just Give Me Jesus*, (Nashville, TN:
W Publishing, 2002).

29. *Hope for Each Day*, Billy Graham, p. 383.
(Nashville, TN: Thomas Nelson, Inc., 2002).

31. *Grace for the Moment,* Max Lucado, p. 742.
Originally from *The Applause of Heaven* (Nashville,
TN: Word, 1990).

33. *God's Way Day by Day,* Charles F. Stanley, p. 38.
(Nashville, TN: Thomas Nelson, Inc., 2004).

35. *Grace for the Moment*, Max Lucado, p. 728.
Originally from *When God Whispers Your Name*
(Nashville, TN: Word, 1994).

36. *Hope for Each Day,* Billy Graham, p. 377.
(Nashville, TN: Thomas Nelson, Inc., 2002).

37. *Grace for the Moment,* Max Lucado, p. 655. Originally from *No Wonder They Call Him the Savior* (Nashville, TN: W Publishing Group, 2003).

38. *The Joy of My Heart*; Anne Graham Lotz, p. 359. Originally from *The Vision of His Glory*, (Nashville, TN: W Publishing, 1996)

39. *Grace for the Moment,* Max Lucado, p. 649. Originally from *God Came Near* (Nashville, TN: W Publishing Group, 2003).